P9-DXG-942

CALGARY PUBLIC LIBRARY

AUG   2017

MY FIRST

Karate Class

By Alyssa Satin Capucilli

Photographs by Leyah Jensen

Ready-to-Read

Simon Spotlight

New York   London   Toronto   Sydney   New Delhi

This book was previously published with slightly different text and art.

For young karate enthusiasts . . . everywhere!

—A.S.C.

To Mikkel, my brother, who was every bit

worth the wait.

—L.J.

SIMON SPOTLIGHT
An imprint of Simon & Schuster Children's Publishing Division
1230 Avenue of the Americas, New York, New York 10020
This Simon Spotlight edition December 2016
Text copyright © 2012 by Alyssa Satin Capucilli
Photographs and illustrations copyright © 2012 by Simon & Schuster, Inc.
For information about special discounts for bulk purchases, please contact Simon & Schuster Special Sales at
1-866-506-1949 or business@simonandschuster.com.
Manufactured in the United States of America 1116 LAK
2 4 6 8 10 9 7 5 3 1
This book has been cataloged with the Library of Congress.
ISBN 978-1-4814-7932-5 (hc)
ISBN 978-1-4814-7931-8 (pbk)
ISBN 978-1-4814-7933-2 (eBook)
This book was previously published with slightly different text and art.

It is my first day
of karate.

My outfit is great to me!

I have a white belt.

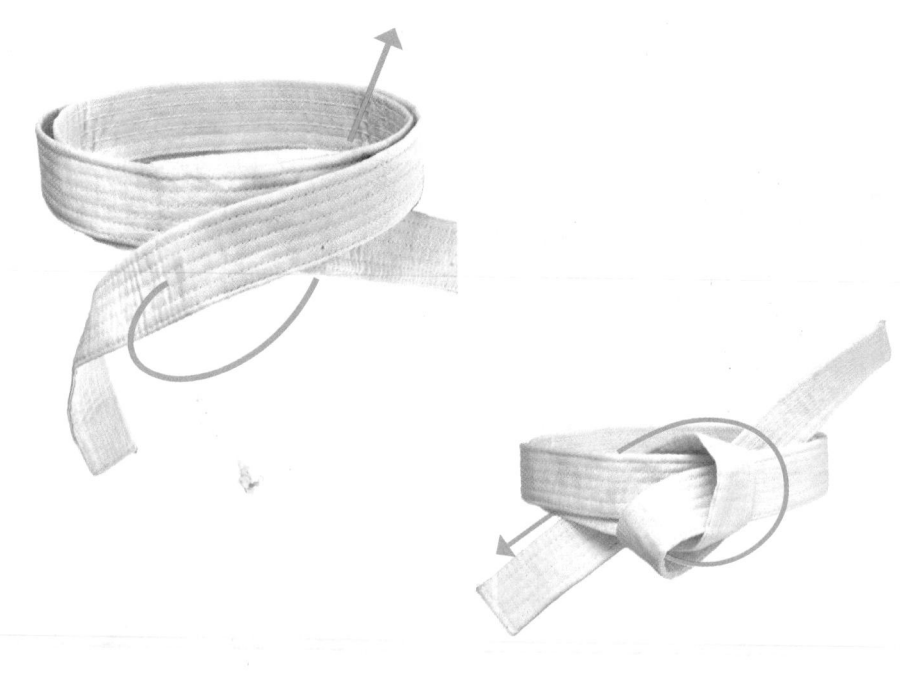

It means I am new.

My uniform is called a gi!

First we take a breath.

Then we make a deep bow
and get our bodies ready.

We stretch and bend
and balance like a crane.

Look at me!

I can stand very steady!

We practice our stance,

a block, and a punch.

We practice big kicks, too!

These are called
katas in karate class.

It is fun to learn
something new!

We prowl like tigers
and slither like snakes.

"Hai ya!"

we say with a cheer.

After one final bow,

it is time for a drink.

I am as thirsty
as a bear!

Sensei says, "Good job!"

Slow and steady is the way!

We get colorful belts
as we learn even more.

I will practice my karate every day!

Do you want to be a karate master?

Find a grown-up to help you learn the karate moves in this book!

Warm Up!

1
Take a Bow

Let's warm up for karate!
Stand with your feet pointing
straight ahead like two train tracks.
Bend forward at the waist to bow.

2 Stretch

Lift your shoulders up and down . . .

and up and down

and up and down again.

That feels great!

3 Bend

Now bend your body
from side to side.
Reach with your arms
and imagine you are
painting a big rainbow.

4 Balance

Stand on one leg with
your fists to the side.
Pretend you are a statue.
Try not to wobble!

Now try the other leg!
You will need this move
again and again in karate class!

Practice Your Katas

1 Stance

Practice makes perfect in karate!
Stand with your feet about shoulder-width apart.

2 Block

Crisscross, applesauce!
Fold both arms and hold your
fists in front of your chest.

Raise one hand over your head
and turn both palms to the sky.
That's a block.

3 Punch

Close both fists. Put one hand near your hip and stretch one hand out in front of you. Now quickly change hands. That's a punch!

4 Kick

Stand on one leg. Touch your heel to your knee. Now kick your leg out in front of you and bring it back in. That's a super karate kick!

Practice!

1 Prowl like a Tiger!

Kneel on all fours.
Can you straighten
both legs with
a powerful roar and
push up?

2 Say "Hai ya"!

"Hai ya" is a great big "YES!" in Japanese.

Haiiiiiiiii

YAAA!

Say it when you do a movement that is just right.

3
Slither Like a Snake

How fast can you scramble on your belly?
Remember, snakes have no hands or feet to help them.

4 Drink Water

Always have a cool
drink of water when
you practice karate.
Yummy!

Practice Makes Perfect

1 Karate Belts

A karate belt is called an obi.
A white obi is for beginners.
There are other colors too,
like yellow, green, blue, and brown.
A black belt means you are an
expert in karate.

2 Slow and Steady

Slowly practice your stance,
block, punch, and kick.
It is important to do it just right.

3
Show Your Karate Moves

You can show your sensei and your friends
how well you are doing your moves.

You may even get
a new belt.
It's exciting!

4
Have Fun!

No matter what color belt you wear, enjoy yourself.

Karate is fun!